W9-CCE-334

small ways to shape our world.

small ways to shape our world.

hardie grant books

Small changes x lots of people = big change

The simple shapes and words in this book explore connection and meaning. They remind us it's the little things that can count most. They add up and often cost you nothing.

They ignite change and make the people around you happier.

So please, as you read, think about reshaping your world with small acts of kindness, thoughtfulness and quiet rebellion.

even
turning
a page can
be an act
of quiet
rebellion.

what
makes you
special?

celebrate what makes us different.

**celebrate
what makes
us the same.**

spend time with someone from a different generation.

why do some cultures have elders but others have the elderly?

theelders.org

share
more
meals
together.

there are
7.5 billion
of us.
how can
anyone be
lonely?

bake
something
for a
neighbour.

bake something for a friend.

sympathy is feeling sorry for someone's pain.

empathy is trying to understand someone's pain.

when did you last read to someone?

**smile
and
smile
back.**

homeless doesn't mean nameless.

thebigissue.org.au

when
you listen,
you give
someone
a voice.

people can change their stripes.

what three things would you take if you had to flee your home?

asrc.org.au (asylum seeker resource centre)

don't overfill the kettle.

**get off
your train
one stop
early.**

who are the traditional owners of your suburb?

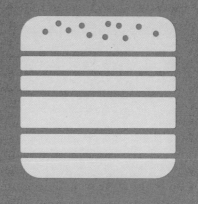

we produce about 4 billion tonnes of food each year. how can anyone be hungry?

foodwise.com.au

buy
nothing
today.

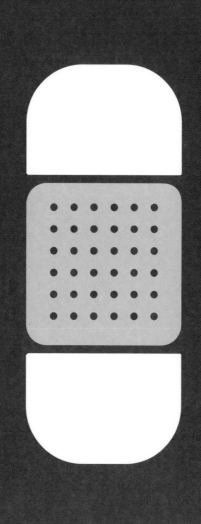

take a pint out for a friend. give blood.

donateblood.com.au

write to someone who inspires you.

the
art of
listening
is about
not
speaking.

there's
every
chance
you're
going to
die.

how
long can
you survive
without
looking at
your
mobile?

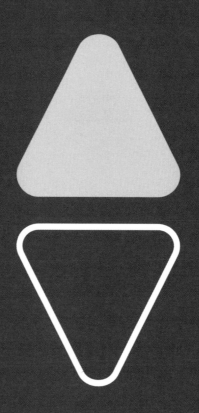

try
saying
hello,
even
in small
spaces.

apple
is also
a fruit.

what you post online is forever.

suicide is a permanent response to what is often a temporary feeling.

lifeline.org.au

is being
a little
different
okay with
you?

how about a lot different?

**people
who need
the most
love often
ask for it
in the most
unlovable
ways.**

no kid dreams of becoming an addict.

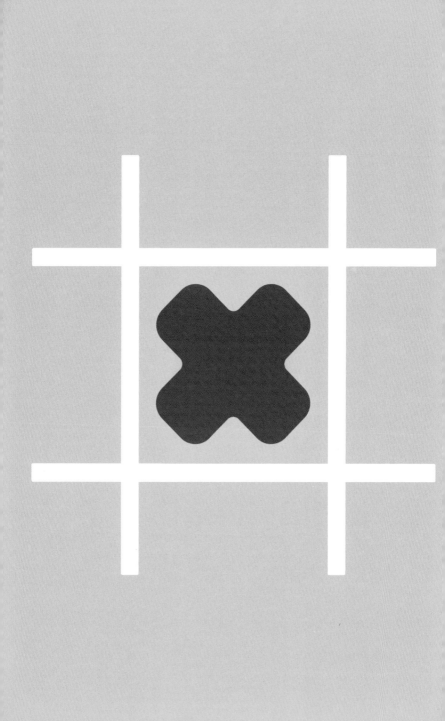

we
are all
only two
moves
away from
being
homeless.

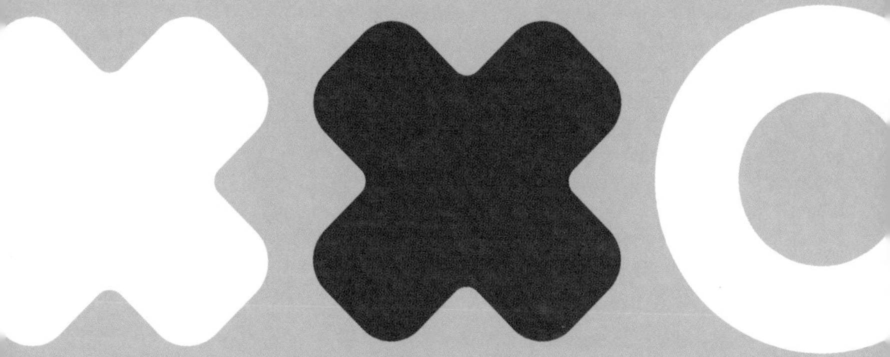

make
love
not
porn.

what if you died and it wasn't a waste?

life
begins
with a
blank
page.

ask, don't assume.

it's good to have worms.

you don't have to be a scientist to save the reef.

oceanservice.noaa.gov/facts/thingsyoucando.html

annoy a moth. kill the lights.

we have
10 million km^3
of fresh water
on earth.
how can
anyone be
thirsty?

**connect
with the land. take a walk.**

**connect
with people.
have a talk.**

what right
do you have
to be here?

what right
do they have
to be here?

think.
act.
pass it on.

what are you waiting for?

As with all Igniting Change initiatives, this book has been made possible by a huge team effort. Many of the ideas in this book come from the courageous individuals and organisations we have the privilege to work with on a daily basis – the quiet rebels!

It was interesting that everyone from whom we sought input said that if they could encourage people just to listen to them without judging them, they felt things would change. If people would stop giving to them but work with them, stop talking about them but talk with them – then they could be part of the change too.

In particular we would like to thank:

TBWA\Melbourne for their design and creative inspiration: Eric Benitez, Pat Sofra, Gavin O'Brien, Kimberlee Wells, Paul Reardon, Rob Hibbert, Emily Watt, Amelia van Veenendaal.

Hardie Grant Books, in particular Sandy Grant and Arwen Summers.

Andrew Anastasios for his craft and wisdom in bringing Igniting Change to life!

The Igniting Change family including the team Anne-Marie Sullivan, Celia Hirsh, Jackie Polonsky, Jacqui Webb, Jane Tewson, Jayde Van Summeren, Linda Fox, Stephanie Exton, David Pledger, Charles Lane, Jess Frid and most importantly the brave people we walk alongside.

The pages include some websites that might be useful resources:

theelders.org
yourenergysavings.gov.au
asrc.org.au
welcometocountry.mobi
buynothingproject.org
thebigissue.org.au
storiesfromtheinside.com.au
donateblood.com.au
thegroundswellproject.com
lifeline.org.au
register.donatelife.gov.au
itstimewetalked.com.au
permaculturenews.org (search worm farm)
un.org/en/universal-declaration-human-rights
oceanservice.noaa.gov

For more information and ideas, please visit ignitingchange.org.au/smallwaystoshapeourworld

Make Love Not Porn is a website started by Cindy Gallop

Published in 2018 by Igniting Change, in conjunction with
Hardie Grant Books, an imprint of Hardie Grant Publishing.

Hardie Grant Books (Melbourne)
Building 1, 658 Church Street
Richmond, Victoria 3121

Hardie Grant Books (London)
5th & 6th Floors
52–54 Southwark Street
London SE1 1UN

ignitingchange.org.au
hardiegrantbooks.com

A Cataloguing-in-Publication entry is available from the
catalogue of the National Library of Australia at www.nla.gov.au

Small ways to shape our world

ISBN 9781743794197

Colour reproduction by Splitting Image Colour Studio

Printed in China by 1010 Printing International Limited

IGNITING CHANGE
by combining extraordinary lives

TBWA\ Melbourne